My Doctor Says

I Have ADHD

written by

Dr C R Yemula

Health insights 4u

Empowering you through knowledge

To my lovely children Nikitha and Nehal

Published in the UK in 2008 by
Health Insights 4U Ltd
60 Bradgate Road
Bedford, UK, MK40 3GB
www.healthinsights4u.com
Email: info@healthinsights4u.com

ISBN 978-0-9558614-4-4
A catalogue record for this book is available
from the British Library

Any product mentioned in the book should be used in
accordance with the prescribing information prepared by the
manufacturer. Neither the author nor the publisher can accept
responsibility for any detrimental consequences arising from
the information contained herein.

Please note:
The information presented in this book is intended as a
support to professional advice and care. It is not a substitute
for a medical diagnosis or treatment.

Contents

Dr Chinnaiah Yemula is a Developmental Paediatrician who works as a Consultant in the community in Bedford. He is employed by Bedfordshire PCT in the United Kingdom. He lives in Bedford with his wife and two children.

He has a special interest in childhood health conditions such as ADHD, behavioural difficulties, epilepsy, bedwetting and developmental problems. In his clinics, he particularly enjoys interacting with children to understand their problems and how best to help them.

He is immensely grateful to children and their parents for being the source of his inspiration and generating the enthusiasm for writing many child-friendly books. He is the author of the following books.

- **Everything a child needs to know about ADHD**
  published by ADDISS, the national ADHD support group, UK, 2nd edition 2007.

- **Everything a child needs to know about Epilepsy**
  published by National Services for Health Improvement, UK, 2008.

- **Everything a child needs to know about Bedwetting**
  published by Health Insights 4U Ltd, UK, 2008.

Dr Yemula would like to thank his friends, colleagues, teachers, parents and lots of children (some of whom have ADHD) for their creative ideas and comments. He sincerely extends his gratitude to the following people.

Children

- Luke, 6 years
- Cameron, 8 years
- Charlie, 9 years
- Connor, 10 years
- Peter, 10 years
- Laura, 11 years
- Matthew, 11 years
- Zack, 11 years

Parents

- Sharon Fuccillo, mother and ADHD Coach
- Alison Barclay
- Natalie Kenney
- Andrea Wheeler

Teachers

- Rekha Patil
- Helen Manley
- Alyson Little
- Liz Bonar

Nurses

- Pam Bordoli
- Josie Minns

Doctors

- Raj Kathane, Child and Adolescent Psychiatrist
- Chris Steer, Consultant Paediatrician
- Adele Humphrey, Consultant Paediatrician
- Professor Frank Besag, Consultant Neuropsychiatrist

Other professionals

- Candis Zenna
- Des Robson
- Kate Marchant
- Karen Meehan
- Sheila Sharples
- Fintan O'Regan, Behaviour Consultant

A note for parents

Dear Parents and Carers,

ADHD is a neuro-developmental condition seen in many school-age children, which is now increasingly recognised by paediatricians, psychiatrists and neurologists worldwide.

Children with ADHD often have difficulties with their behaviour, family relations, friendships and academic achievement. Living with ADHD can cause great stress within and outside the family.

As a parent and carer, you may need to try various strategies to manage your child's behavioural and academic difficulties.

Whilst a vast amount of information is available for adults about ADHD, there is an ongoing need for good quality child-friendly literature. I hope this book goes some way towards filling this gap and assists in educating children about various aspects of ADHD.

Please read this book with your child and discuss their problems in a relaxed and friendly way.

Best wishes,

Chinnaiah Yemula

A note for children

Dear Boys and Girls,

This is the story of Buzz, a 9-year-old boy, who has ADHD. ADHD is a medical condition that is seen in many school-age children all over the world.

Don't feel bad if you have ADHD. It is not your fault. Remember, you are not alone. There are thousands of children in the UK with this medical condition.

Buzz would like to share his story with you all, so that you can get to know all about ADHD, learn from his mistakes and do better at home and at school.

You can read this book at your own pace and in stages. Share your ideas and thoughts with your brothers, sisters, friends and also the grown-ups at home.

Good luck and best wishes,

Chinnaiah Yemula

Hi Boys and Girls!

My name is Buzz

Welcome to my story. I would like you to come and join me as I go through my journey with ADHD. You may be wondering what this is all about. Well, you need to stay with me until the end of the story. I promise you will find out lots of information about this condition called ADHD.

When you start reading this book, it will be like a roller coaster ride, but it is in your hands and you can stop and start wherever you wish. It is nice to be in control, right? Don't we all secretly wish we could be in charge of everything all the time?

About me

Here are some facts about me. Maybe some of you will share my likes and dislikes! You will learn even more about me as you read this book, but remember, not everyone behaves as I did.

Age:	9 years old
Height:	1.2 metres
Eye colour:	Blue
Hair colour:	Black
School:	Smart Valley Primary School
I love:	Drawing, playing football and computer games
My favourite football team:	Victors United
I hate:	My Dad snoring at night and the taste of brussel sprouts. Yuck!
Girl I fancy:	Come on, why would I tell you that?

Now, let me introduce you to my family.

Dad Danny

Mum Monica

This is my Dad Danny

Age: 36 years old

Job: Manager at a leisure centre

Loves: Food, movies and coaching football to young children at the weekends

Hates: His bulging tummy

Supports: The local football club – Victors United

I like going out with Dad to play football at the weekends. Sometimes we go to the cinema and have lots of fun.

This is my lovely Mum Monica

Age: 34 years old (but keep this to yourself, Mum will get cross if you tell anybody at your school)

Job: Full time Mum

Loves: Cooking. I am very proud of my Mum and I think she is the best cook in the world

Hates: A dirty kitchen

Supports: The football club – Pride City

My Mum loves me to bits but keeps nagging me all the time!

Meet my family

Brother Ben

This is my brother Ben

Age: Nearly 6 years old but acts like a baby

Likes: Watching cricket, eating ice cream and chocolates.

Annoying habit: Very bossy and he always beats me to the toilet

Clever about: Convincing my Dad that he is right and I am wrong

Supports: The English cricket team.

Sister Sophie

Here is my sister Sophie

Age: Only 11 years old but thinks she is a grown-up

Annoying habit: Very demanding and picks on me all the time (particularly when Dad is not around)

Likes: Talking for ages to her friends on her mobile!

Hates: Spicy food and smelly socks, especially mine!

Supports: The football club – Pride City.

Grandad George

This is my cool Grandad

Age: 66 years old

Job: Retired, but was the Head Teacher of Long Story Primary School. No wonder, he is the best story teller

Likes: Playing golf and doing crosswords

Hates: Losing his hair

I love him very much. He is kind and caring. I like to go to my Grandad's house every weekend (if I have my way).

Nan Nancy

Here is my Nan

Age: 63 years old

Works: At a local charity shop two days a week

Likes: Walking the dog, music and dancing

Hates: The house being messy

We all love Nan because she is very kind and generous, particularly with chocolates and sweets.

When I was little

My Nan says...

I started to get into trouble when I turned two. I was into everything at home. Somebody had to keep an eye on me 24 hours a day - that is 1,440 minutes or 86,400 seconds a day! My Mum couldn't leave me anywhere on my own even for 5 minutes. No wonder she got tired!

I was naughty and very noisy. I used to scream at the top of my voice if anybody said 'NO' to me. Obviously, this word didn't exist in my dictionary. I never did as I was told.

Scary bathroom

My Mum used to call me a 'Cheeky Monkey' all the time. One day, I was in the bath and was messing about as usual. Mum was in the bathroom arranging towels and putting laundry in the bin. Nan was downstairs in the kitchen getting my sister ready for breakfast.

Suddenly, I screamed and Mum looked at me to find out what was wrong. My index finger was stuck in the plughole in the bath! Mum tried to get it out and I was yelling in pain.

Mum called for help and Nan came rushing in. In the end, Mum pulled my finger out but it was a bit swollen. She then put some cream on it and gave me a medicine for the pain.

After a while I calmed down. Mum says I was scared afterwards and cried a lot whenever I went into the bath. This went on for at least six months.

Messy in the kitchen

Nan says I was always on the go and never sat still for a second. I would go into the kitchen, get on the stool and climb onto the worktop to get to the top shelf. This is where I had fun. I would empty the salt pot, gravy granules and anything else I could find. This happened a lot and my poor Mum had to clean up the mess.

Looking back, I marvel at my amazing climbing skills. Perhaps I will be a famous mountaineer one day.

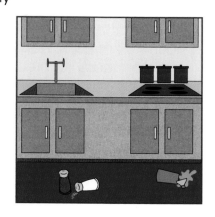

Mum told me I threw really bad tantrums when I was three years old. At the supermarket, I would run between the aisles, shouting and touching everything on the shelves. So Mum stopped taking me out.

At home, whenever I got cross, I would go to a CD rack in the living room and throw CDs, one by one, from the bottom shelf. For some reason, I never went for the books in the bookcase – maybe they were too heavy to pick up and throw. I used to run around the house crying.

When I stopped crying, Dad made me pick up all the CDs and put them back on the CD rack. Because I felt so tired after a tantrum, Dad said I sometimes fell asleep on the floor.

Naughty at the Nursery

I went to the 'Bezee Bees' nursery. Mum told me I was very clingy and always wanted her to sit with me in the big hall. Whenever I was dropped off in the morning, I used to scream for at least half an hour and could not be consoled. I would then settle down to play with other children, but on my terms only.

Mrs Rush

At the nursery, I would push the other children and never let anyone take my soft toys. Mrs Rush, the nursery nurse said I was very naughty and would grab somebody's toy and not let go of it for hours. Soon, parents of other children started complaining about my behaviour. I was on the go and never sat in one place for more than a couple of minutes. I threw tantrums if anyone said 'No' to me.

One day, I was so upset, I went to the huge toy box in the middle of the room and started throwing the toys at everybody. I kept on screaming and Mrs Rush had to take all the children out of the room. Then, she rang my parents to come and pick me up. "Oh dear, Buzz is making trouble again!" they exclaimed.

Now I want to tell you what generally happens at my house. Mum tries to wake me up at around 7 o'clock, but I hate getting up early. I just like to stay in bed and sleep more. Mum says mornings are very busy and she never knows what mood I will be in first thing.

Then Mum keeps nagging me to brush my teeth, take a shower and dress quickly for school. When I get cross I scream a lot and push Mum out of the bathroom.

Sometimes, she has to chase me whilst I run around the bedrooms before I get dressed. Mum says I am a bit clumsy. I do up my buttons the wrong way and struggle with my shoelaces. Of course, Mum helps me a lot and also packs my school bag and PE kit.

Dad says I'm a 'scatterbrain'. I sometimes forget to take my lunch box and school books in the mornings. Poor Dad, he has to drive back to my school to drop them off. Mum gets cross because I lose lots of things at school – like my PE kit, pencil case and even my lunch box.

I can't stay in one place. I run around the house all the time. Even when I watch my favourite DVD, I fidget, walk up and down and fiddle with the remote control. Mum says that I have 'ants in my pants'.

I get easily annoyed and lose my temper if I don't get what I want. Nan says Sophie and Ben don't like inviting their friends to our house as I can be really nasty and a big nuisance.

When I get home from school, I go upstairs to the bathroom for a wash and get changed. Mum gives me an apple or orange as a snack, which I don't like at all. I always ask for crisps or a chocolate bar instead but Mum says it's much healthier to have fruit every day.

After dinner, Mum makes me sit at the table to do my homework. I don't like doing it because it's hard and I mess it up a lot. I get bored after doing just 2 or 3 pages and can't concentrate any more. If Mum is not with me, I leave the table to watch TV or go on the computer to play games.

Angry outbursts

When I do my homework, I want to know the stuff straight away. If I don't, I get so angry; I rip the book, throw it down and storm off. I feel sorry afterwards and apologise to Mum. I don't know why I get so angry and frustrated. I can't help it.

Even worse, Sophie laughs at my writing and says it is a terrible mess! Mum tells her off but I know I can't write very well and make lots of mistakes. I get bored really quickly and wish I didn't have to do stinky homework!

Every Saturday evening, we sit down in the living room and play family games together. My favourite one is Bingo. Of course, I must always win in the end. If I don't get a full house, I get angry, shout and cry and then knock the game onto the floor.

I hate losing
any games!
I must always win,
no matter what!

Tantrums at home

I once had a horrible day at school getting into trouble, yet again. When I got home, I was feeling angry so I threw my bag across the hall and my coat on the floor. Mum was cross and asked me to pick them up. I said "No". So she said I had to go to my room until I was ready to pick them up.

I then ran upstairs shouting horrible things and started banging on the bedroom door. When I calmed down, I felt sorry for what I had done.

Hospital visit

My Nan says I have lots of accidents as I am always in a rush and do things without any fear of danger. Last Christmas, we were playing and having fun in our bedroom. Suddenly, I climbed on to the top bunk bed and jumped down. I hit my head on the edge of a table and started crying because it really hurt and my forehead was bleeding. Mum took me to the hospital and I needed 3 stitches on my forehead. "Thank goodness, it wasn't more serious," said Mum.

Trouble playing football

Every Sunday we go to the local club near our house to play football. Once I was running towards the goal to kick the ball and score. Suddenly, Danny, who was the goalie for the other side, came and grabbed it. It was so unfair and I pushed him. He then pushed me so I kicked him.

The referee came and demanded an apology. I refused. We began playing football again but soon I lost my temper and kicked two other players. I was then banned from playing football again. I felt sorry afterwards but it was too late!

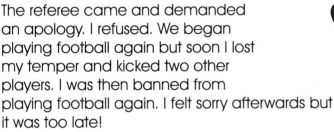

During the Easter holidays, my Dad's friend invited us for a barbeque party at his home. In the garden, I was playing football with Ben and his friends. Ben got in the way while I was tackling the ball and I fell down.

I got up and saw Ben laughing at me. I got very angry and punched and kicked him. He started crying so everybody came rushing to find out what was happening. Dad then made me say sorry to my brother. Mum was very embarrassed and said she would never take me out again because I was so naughty.

About my school

I should now tell you about my school – Smart Valley Primary School. The school is about 15 minutes' drive from our house but it takes longer during the rush hour. However, there is a shortcut and I can get to school in 10 minutes if I walk fast through a small alleyway. I'm always in a hurry and run to school, especially if I'm late.

This is our Head Teacher, Mr Quickstep. He is always at the main gate first thing in the morning, greeting all the children arriving at school. He is very strict and expects children to behave well in his school.

Mr Quickstep

Let me introduce our class teacher, Mrs Hurrey. She is a lovely teacher who is kind and caring. She often stutters if she is stressed, especially if the children are very noisy in the classroom (this includes me).

Mrs Hurrey

I like Maths lessons very much but I am not so sure about English. I hate spelling tests, especially when I have to spell long words like 'attention' or 'detention'.

I often make silly mistakes and my handwriting is messy. I rush so much that sometimes I can't read what I have written. "You know if you slow down and take care, you can write a lot better," said Mrs Hurrey.

"Buzz, you made lots of mistakes in Maths," said Mrs Hurrey. "I know you love Maths. I can see you have worked hard today. Just make sure you check your answers once you completed them." Mrs Hurrey then showed me the notebook with my homework in it.

I have a Maths lesson every day before lunch. One day, Mrs Hurrey was explaining about addition and subtraction. Somebody dropped a pencil on the carpet. I picked it up and started fiddling with it. I just couldn't concentrate and I soon started tapping the floor with my shoe.

"Buzz, please stop making that noise and be quiet," said Mrs Hurrey. I kept quiet for a little while. I then started shouting out the answers. "Buzz, put your hand up before you say anything," reminded Mrs Hurrey, gently. I then made a paper ball and threw it at Tom, who sat at the front of the class. All the children were laughing at me and, of course, I was enjoying the attention.

Mrs Hurrey was annoyed when I got up and started walking around the classroom. "Buzz, you are disturbing the whole class," said Mrs Hurrey. I was then asked to leave the room. I was sent to the 'Thinking Room'. I felt sorry for what I did but deep down, I knew I just couldn't help it. I am 'full of beans'.

Fighting in the playground

I love playtime. We run around in the playground and play 'Stuck in the Mud'. It's a very popular game at our school. To start the game, someone is named 'IT', which means he or she has to run after everyone else who is playing. If the person who is 'IT' tags someone else, that person has to stand still, like a statue, with their arms and legs spread.

One day, we were playing the game and Tom was made 'IT'. He came and tagged me so I had to stand still. I was restless because no one was coming to free me. I started to argue with Tom to change the rules. He didn't agree with me so I pushed him onto the grass.

Just then, the bell rang and we walked towards the science room. Suddenly, Tom pushed my books out of my hands. I got angry and punched him in his stomach. We began fighting and the teacher came rushing over and made us apologise to each other.

My parents were told that I was continuously misbehaving at school and so I was excluded (kept out of school) for a day. Yes, I was in trouble once again!

After about 6 weeks, Mr Quickstep, the Head teacher, called my parents to the school. He wanted to talk about my behaviour. He told them that he was very concerned about the way I was behaving in the classroom. He told my parents that:

- I make lots of noise and distract the other children in the classroom. I talk a lot and shout out the answers.

- I often fight in the playground.

- I don't listen to the teachers and I answer back all the time.

- I often get up and walk around the classroom during the lesson.

- I don't pay attention and constantly tap on the floor.

- I am poorly organised and very forgetful.

Mr Quickstep also said that I am behind with my schoolwork and not achieving good grades. He asked my parents to see our family doctor to find out if I have any medical problems.

The next day, Mum made an appointment to see our family doctor. She picked me up from school and we went straight to see Dr Smart at the surgery.

Mum told Dr Smart that I am very naughty, both at home and school. Mum said it is very stressful having to cope with my behaviour at home.

Dr Smart then wrote a letter to Dr Best, asking him to see me in the clinic.

Dear Dr Best,

Re: Buzz

Could you please see this delightful 9-year-old boy in your clinic as soon as possible?

Buzz seems to have lots of behavioural problems both at home and school. His parents are keen to find out if he has any medical problems, such as ADHD.

Yours sincerely

Dr Smart

Dr Smart

I went to see Dr Best

Mum told me that Dr Best is a paediatrician, which means a special doctor for children, and that he sees lots of children with behavioural difficulties.

I thought he would be an old doctor with a bald head, a grey moustache and wearing thick glasses on his long nose. I went with Mum and Dad to see Dr Best at his clinic. Dad took time off work for the appointment and I was glad to be out of school for the whole afternoon.

It was a bright sunny day and we arrived at the clinic just before the appointment. The receptionist smiled at me and asked us to sit in the waiting area. It was a lovely big hall with lots of children's books, puzzles and toys.

In a corner there was a small TV and guess what was on? The Simpsons. My favourite programme! I grabbed the remote control and started increasing the volume. Mum asked me not to fiddle with the remote control but I was too excited to stop and listen.

What did Dr Best do?

After a while, Dr Best came to the waiting room and called out my name. I was surprised to see a young doctor walking towards us. He shook hands with Mum, Dad and me.

We followed Dr Best into his clinic room. It was a huge room with two lovely pictures on the wall and a big table in the corner. Dr Best sat next to the table and took notes while he spoke to my parents.

Dr Best asked, "Well, Buzz, would you like to draw some pictures or do some puzzles while I speak to your Mum and Dad?" I replied, "Thank you Dr Best, I would love that." I then sat by the side of a tiny table and began colouring in the pictures.

Dr Best asked Mum and Dad about my behaviour at home and school. He looked at my school report and read what my teacher had written about me.

- Buzz can't sit still and talks non-stop
- He is very disruptive and answers back in class
- He could do better if only he paid more attention

How I behaved at the clinic

I got very bored sitting still at the table. I got up, walked to the window and tried to pull the curtains down. Then I hid behind the curtains for a short while before I went to the washbasin and turned on the taps. "Buzz, stop running around the clinic," shouted Mum. I ignored her.

I then went to the big table and began playing with Dr Best's stethoscope. Dad asked me to stop fiddling with it. Dr Best looked anxious as I almost dropped it but, luckily, Dad caught it.

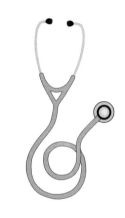

Dr Best asked me lots of questions about how I was doing at school, about my friends and whether I get along well with Ben and Sophie at home. I picked up a rubber band and kept playing with it as I was answering the questions.

I told Dr Best that I seem to have lots of things going on in my head. He was interested to hear that I often sat on my hands to stop them from moving. I agreed that I'm naughty sometimes, but it isn't my fault. I also told Dr Best that at home Ben never leaves me alone and is always trying to wind me up.

Dr Best then asked Mum and Dad lots of questions about my birth details, my behaviour when I was little and about my development. He gave me a thorough check-up and said I was in good health.

Mum and Dad had heard about ADHD and asked Dr Best whether I had this condition. Dr Best nodded and said gently, "Yes, Buzz has ADHD and this is why he has lots of behavioural difficulties at home and school."

Mum said, "We now know why Buzz is the way he is and I can now tell other people that he is not a naughty boy but has ADHD." Dr Best said it is important for everybody, including my teachers, friends and family members, to understand more about my condition.

Dr Best told me that ADHD is a short name
for a medical condition called
'Attention Deficit Hyperactivity Disorder'.
This sounds very complicated! Many adults,
even some clever children (like me)
find it difficult to say the full name
as it can be a real tongue-twister!
Anyway, let's just call it ADHD from now on.

Mr Curlytongue

Some people say ADHD doesn't
exist and is just another name for
naughtiness. This is not true. Dr Best
said that scientists have studied lots
of school-age children all over the world
and identified certain difficulties with behaviour
that are only seen in children with ADHD.

Did you know?

ADHD can occur in
children from different
backgrounds and places
such as America, Africa,
Europe and Asia.

Dr Best said that ADHD is not a new problem and it has been around for thousands of years. Heinrich Hoffmann, a German doctor, was the first person to write a book of poems about 'Fidgety Philip' in 1845. Philip was a naughty and hyperactive lad.

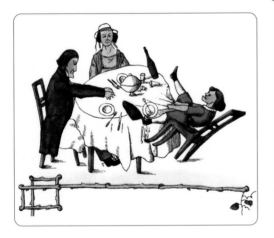

"Let me see if Philip can
Be a little gentleman;
Let me see, if he is able
To sit still for once at table:
Thus Papa bade Phil behave;
And Mamma looked very grave.
But fidgety Phil,
He won't sit still;
He wriggles
And giggles,
And then, I declare,
Swings backwards and forwards
And tilts up his chair,
Just like any rocking horse;-
"Philip! I am getting cross!"

In 1902, George Still, a British doctor, wrote about a group of children with hyperactivity and short attention span.

So, boys and girls, perhaps our great, great grandparents might have had ADHD too! Still, they didn't have remote controls to play with and I wonder what things they might have fiddled with when they got bored!

What does ADHD mean?

Dr Best said that children with ADHD often have many problems at home and at school. Most children with ADHD have a combination of difficulties in all 3 areas of ADHD –
A. Inattention B. Hyperactivity C. Impulsiveness

Box A   Inattention

- Make careless mistakes in school work
- Have great difficulty concentrating on the tasks
- Easily distracted
- Forgetful and lose things

Box B   Hyperactivity

- On the go as if driven by a motor
- Restless and can't sit still
- Fidgety
- Walks about in the classroom

Box C   Impulsiveness

- Talk a lot
- Have great difficulty waiting for their turn in games and tend to interrupt conversations
- Blurt out the answer before the question is completed

Three types of ADHD

Doctor Best said that most children have what is called a 'Combined type of ADHD'. This means they have difficulties in all the three areas of ADHD.

Some children, especially girls, tend to have an 'Inattentive type of ADHD'. It is also called 'Attention Deficit Disorder'. These children have poor concentration and a short attention span.

There are some children who are quite overactive as well as impulsive and have a 'Hyperactive / Impulsive type of ADHD'.

ADHD

Inattentive type	Hyperactive/ Impulsive type	Combined type
See Box A on page 36	**See Boxes B+C** on page 36	**See Boxes A+B+C** on page 36

How common is ADHD?

Dr Best said there are lots of children like me who have ADHD and are struggling at home and school. You may see one child with ADHD in every class of 25 to 30 children at school. However, only one child out of 100 children tends to have the most difficulties with ADHD.

Did you know that both boys and girls can have ADHD? It is, however, more common in boys. ADHD is also seen in teenagers and some adults.

Co-existing problems

"Some children with ADHD also have other problems," said Dr Best. They are as follows:

Being clumsy
•
Poor handwriting

Stubborn
•
Annoying
•
Arguing a lot

Lying
•
Stealing
•
Fighting

Learning difficulties

Difficulty making and keeping friends

Can you test for ADHD?

My Mum asked Dr Best if there are any blood tests
to check if I have ADHD. I wouldn't mind having
some tests and I'm cool when it comes to blood tests,
unlike my brother Ben.

Dr Best replied that there is no special test as yet to
confirm children with ADHD. However, some children
may need special tests to find out if they have any other
medical or educational problems.

Does ADHD run in families?

My dad wondered if ADHD runs in families. Dr Best said
ADHD can be passed on to children from their parents
and grandparents. He also said that we get certain
ADHD genes from both our parents that
can cause problems which we see in
children with ADHD.

I asked, "Dr Best, I have 2 pairs of jeans
at home. Shall I throw them away,
just in case?" Dr Best smiled and said,
"I meant genes, not jeans. Genes are
tiny blocks of information that we all
carry in our body cells."

More about genes

Genes are things that make us the way we are –
for example, the colour of our hair and eyes
as well as certain types of behaviour.
"If you have ADHD, you can blame the
genes but not your parents!"
said Dr Best.

What causes ADHD?

"Scientists have been working hard to figure
out what exactly causes ADHD," said
Dr Best. He explained that we all have
certain chemicals in the brain to help us
behave well. They also help us to
understand the messages coming from
our brain correctly.

Children with ADHD tend to have low
levels of these chemicals in their brains. As
a result, they find it too hard to understand
and manage their thoughts. "It's like having your home
telephone badly connected and therefore you can't hear
or talk properly," said Dr Best. "But remember, ADHD is not
caused by a bad diet or poor parenting skills."

Mum and Dad were worried about my ADHD. They asked Dr Best if ADHD can be cured and whether I can get rid of it once and for all.

"It is not like a common cold which you have for only a short period," said Dr Best. "ADHD is a condition you have for a long time, just like diabetes or asthma. Although we can't get rid of ADHD, we can do lots of things to help children do well both at home and at school."

He went on to explain that children, as well as their parents and teachers, need to understand more about ADHD. Dr Best then talked about certain things that my parents and teacher can do to help my behaviour.

He gave Mum and Dad some leaflets about ADHD. He said he would send my details and some leaflets to my teacher so that she would understand why I misbehave in class. Help is coming at last!

"But remember, Buzz, ADHD is not an excuse to misbehave and do whatever you like!" Dr Best warned me gently.

"Children with ADHD can have challenging behaviour",
said Dr Best. "They are often stubborn and refuse to
follow instructions. There are many things that parents
can do to help their child's behaviour."

Tips for parents...

- Be consistent and maintain a firm attitude all the time.

- Have a regular routine.

- Set clear rules and boundaries.

- Use reward charts and agree rewards with your child for completing tasks.

- Try 'Time Out' with the child and send him to his bedroom in case he misbehaves.

- Be patient and keep trying!

How can the teacher help?

Dr Best said there are lots of things that my teacher can do to help me perform well at school.

Mrs Goodcare

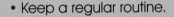

Tips for teachers...

- Keep a regular routine.

- Give clear and simple instructions and make sure the child understands them.

- Give one target at a time and keep the tasks short and snappy.

- Have the child sit close to the teacher and give visual cues in case the child is misbehaving.

- It may be helpful for the child to fiddle with a small rubbery toy in the classroom.

- Be patient and give lots of HELP!

My Mum and Dad asked "Dr Best, can Buzz take a medicine to help him calm down and pay more attention?" "Yes," said Dr Best.
"There are some special medicines to help children with ADHD."

Remember, children with ADHD tend to have low levels of certain chemicals in their brains. Dr Best said the medicine helps to get the chemicals back to normal levels. As a result, children with ADHD are able to sit still and concentrate on tasks.

Dr Best looked at me and smiled.
"Buzz, it's not a magic pill or a magic wand. It certainly doesn't fix all the troubles you have at home and school."

He went on to say, "The medicine is like having 'glasses' for your brain. This will help you to calm down, stay on task and think clearly before you rush and do things. Of course, you still need to listen carefully and work hard."

"However, not all children need to take medicine," said Dr Best. "Medicine is given to children with ADHD who have lots of problems both at home and at school."

Dad asked Dr Best to tell us a bit more about the medicines for ADHD. Dr Best said there are different medicines that can be used for children with ADHD and behavioural problems.

Medicines generally have names which are not easy to say, even for grown-ups! They come as tablets or capsules. Most children don't have any problem swallowing the medicine.

Here are the names of some medicines.

Goodness gracious! I can't say these names!

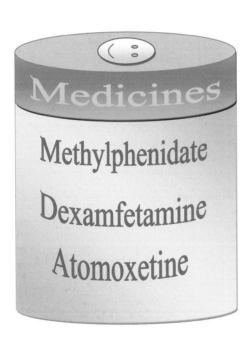

Medicines

Methylphenidate

Dexamfetamine

Atomoxetine

Mr Cleverwords

Dr Best talked about how the medicine can help children and said many children do well after taking it.

How does a medicine help?

- Helps calm you down

- Helps you to sit still and concentrate

- Helps you to think before you act

Mr B Calm

There are some medicines that only work for 3 to 4 hours, therefore the child needs to take the medicine 2 or 3 times a day – at breakfast time, lunch time and late afternoon.

Long-acting medicines

"Are there any medicines for ADHD that work for longer periods?" Dad asked.

Dr Best replied, "Yes, thanks to the hard work of our scientists, we now have several long-acting medicines to help children with ADHD.

There are some medicines that can work for up to 8 hours, one medicine that works for 12 hours and another medicine which can work all day.

The convenience of taking a long-acting medicine is you can take it just once a day in the morning. Like any other medicines, they have long names which are difficult to say.

Some children need to take the medicine every day, while others can stop taking it at weekends. But, Buzz if you have any doubts, you should always check with Mum and Dad about the medicine."

Are there any problems?

My Dad wondered if the medicine causes any problems. Dr Best said, like any other medicine, a medicine for ADHD has lots of benefits but can also cause a few problems. These are called 'side-effects'.

Some children may not eat well and other children may have difficulty getting to sleep at night. However, most children taking the medicine do well and don't have these problems.

Buzz, don't worry!
We can adjust the dose or change the medicine if you have any side-effects.

Dr Best

How to make friends

Dr Best asked my Mum if I have any friends at school. Mum said that I didn't have any friends because I am often rude and fight with other children.

Dr Best then arranged for us to see a special nurse at the hospital. He said she would give me lots of ideas about how to make friends.

A week later I went with Mum to see Mrs Wise. She shook hands with me and sat next to me while I drew some pictures. She asked me about my friends and how I get into little squabbles. I told her I feel very sad because I don't have any friends and I don't get invited to other children's birthday parties. Of course, I'd love to have lots of friends.

Mrs Wise

How to make friends

Mrs Wise gave me a list of things to do and said I can make lots of friends and also keep them if I follow these tips every day.

Ten tips for making friends

1 Say something nice to your friends. Be nice to them and don't tease or call them names. Good friends are kind and caring.

2 Share your ideas and toys when playing with your friends. Have clear rules before playing a game and stick to them.

3 Think twice before you say anything and try not to be rude.

4 Say you are sorry if you hurt others.

5 Be flexible and listen to your friends. It doesn't have to be your way all the time.

6 Find people who like you for being you.

7 Show your friends kindness and respect.

8 Be supportive when they need help.

9 Be truthful, but be kind about it.

10 Ask for help from grown-ups
when needed (Mum, Dad, teacher etc).

How to be well organised

- Have a routine. Make a list of things you need to do every day.

- Always check your list and try not to lose it!

- Write down the things you must remember to do.
- Use a calendar, coloured tabs, cards or 'post its'.

Max Mayhem

- Everything has its place. Use labels for your stuff in drawers or boxes.

- You can then find things easily!

- Check your personal stuff – pencil case, PE kit, lunch box, locker keys etc. at the close of school each day.

"Children with ADHD can be very creative," said Mrs Wise. "Here is a poem written by Connor, a 9-year-old boy with ADHD, who has made lots of friends."

School poem

School is great
And at art we used a lot of paint

I like playtime
I don't like lunchtime

When it is maths I do a lot of work
At playtime I play football with my friends

School is cool, a time to
work and play!

Oh No!
Somebody has been naughty
Here comes the Headmaster,
What a disaster!

After coming home, I couldn't wait to read all about ADHD. At first I was scared to know that I have this medical condition and that other children may tease me if they find out. At bedtime, Mum helped me read a children's book about ADHD. After reading the book, I discovered I'm not alone and that there are lots of children like me with ADHD.

The next day, Mum and Dad were downstairs in the living room watching a TV programme.
"Dad, it's not my fault," I said quietly.
Dad turned back and looked worried.
"What! Have you broken something?"
"No," I said. I showed him the book. "I have read this book about ADHD and it says having ADHD is not your fault."
"Yes, Buzz, you're right," said Dad. "But, you need plenty of help to stop you getting into trouble."

I now understand a lot about ADHD. I have learnt that having ADHD is not an excuse to misbehave or fight with other children. Mum and Dad have also read a book about ADHD and then went to a special 'Parent Training Group' to find out how best to help me at home.

One Saturday, after having a tasty dinner, we all sat down in the living room. Mum told Ben and Sophie that I have ADHD and explained a bit about what it means. Ben and Sophie had lots of doubts. I was happy to lend them my book about ADHD.

"Listen everybody," said Dad. "We are going to have a 'behaviour contract' at home. It means we can all agree on some ground rules of good behaviour and stick to them every day."

"But Dad, what's a contract?" asked Ben. Dad smiled and said "Good question. A contract means you agree to do certain things and sign a paper to confirm that you will do them."

We were all quite excited about the contract but more about our rewards if we followed the rules every day. There are 4 simple rules.

CONTRACT

CONTRACT

- No shouting
- If annoyed, tell Mum and Dad but no fighting
- Keep your bedroom nice and tidy
- Say sorry if you are wrong

Signed

I choose my own rewards for being good for a whole week. Guess what? I can either watch my favourite DVD or have an extra half an hour on the PlayStation.

I was still very hyperactive and continued to get into trouble. I was also lagging behind with my school work, so Mum and Dad wanted me to try an ADHD medicine. Of course, I know how the medicine helps children with ADHD and I agreed to take the medicine. It was so easy taking the medicine in the morning.

After a while, I felt calmer and got ready for school without making too much fuss. After school, I could pay a lot more attention and complete my homework. Dad was surprised that I could sit still and didn't quarrel with anyone when we played board games in the evenings. I felt it was really great having fun with everybody at home.

I go to Nan and Grandad's house every Friday after school. Grandad and I take the dog out for a long walk. I love being with my grandparents and always have lots of fun.

After 3 months... Mrs Hurrey says that I am a lot calmer at school. I now sit close to the teacher and at the very front of the class. Mrs Hurrey gives me small chunks of work to do, one at a time. She knows I can't cope if I am given too many tasks in one go.

In the classroom, I am able stay still for longer and don't fiddle with pencils anymore. I put my hand up before answering any questions. Hurrah! I have neater handwriting now.

At the close of school, I check my PE kit and pencil case to make sure I don't lose any personal belongings. Dad says I'm not a 'scatterbrain' anymore.

I have lots of friends now. In the playground, I follow the rules and don't try to change them in the middle of the game. I hardly cause any trouble when I play with my friends.

Mrs Hurrey gives me a 'Gold star' every week when I do well at school. I now have a huge collection of 'Gold stars'!

 ### ACHIEVEMENT AWARD

- Good behaviour   • Hard work
  - Being a good friend
  Buzz, well done!

From Mr Quickstep

I am what I am

After one year... I take the medicine every day. Ben and Sophie know all about my condition. They are careful not to wind me up when I am in a bad mood. I am much calmer now and rarely cause trouble. Of course, we do get into little arguments sometimes, especially when watching a football match between Victors United and Pride City.

I was allowed back into the local club and enjoy playing football over the weekends. We all play as a team and I rarely get into trouble. I love being with my mates. The great news is that I have been selected as a striker for a football match next week.

We are a happy and fun-loving family. We will be flying to Disneyland in Florida during the summer holidays. I am going to invite all of my friends for my birthday party in September. We are going to have lots of food, fun and much more.

Best wishes and tons of love…

From Buzz

Quiz

Dear Boys and Girls

Buzz has prepared a quiz for you and he would like to test your knowledge about ADHD. There are ten questions and each correct answer carries 10 points.

1 What does ADHD stand for?

A - - - - - - - - - D - - - - - - H - - - - - - - - - - - - - D - - - - - - -

2 ADHD happens in boys only

a) True   b) False

3 Name 3 things a child with ADHD may have

a)-------------------- b) ------------------- c)-----------------------

4 ADHD is just another name for naughtiness

a) True   b) False

5 Name 3 places where ADHD causes trouble

a)-------------------- b) ------------------- c)-----------------------

Quiz

Oops! Buzz forgot to say this – you can't ask or phone a friend in the middle of the quiz to get the answers.

6 Name 2 ways to keep friends

a) ---
b)---

7 Adults don't get ADHD

a) True   b) False

8 Name a medicine for ADHD

M – – – – – ph – – – – – te

9 How does a medicine help?

----

10 Name 2 tips for good behaviour

a) ---
b)---

Answers on page 64

Can you find your way?

Answers on page 64

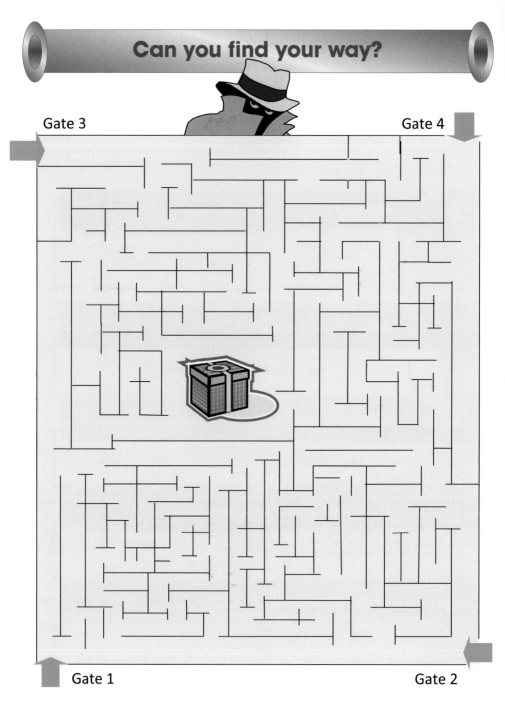

Gate 3

Gate 4

Gate 1

Gate 2

Can you colour these pictures?

Which one are you? Can you colour the words?

Creative Cheeky Happy
Artistic Enthusiastic FUN
Clever Kind Caring

Spot the ten differences

Answers on page 64

Word search

E	V	I	T	C	A	R	E	P	Y	H
S	K	S	Y	T	H	G	U	A	N	Y
C	R	N	C	F	N	A	E	T	A	T
H	O	R	E	H	C	A	E	T	F	I
T	W	D	F	Y	O	F	S	E	R	V
P	E	H	D	P	T	O	C	N	I	I
A	M	P	A	C	O	A	L	T	E	S
F	O	D	A	L	A	S	I	I	N	L
T	H	A	S	R	O	T	C	O	D	U
D	O	T	P	E	N	P	N	N	S	P
M	E	D	I	C	I	N	E	D	E	M
F	R	I	D	M	O	H	P	P	M	I

Hyperactive	School	Homework
Impulsivity	Teacher	Naughty
Attention	Friends	Doctors
ADHD	Pencil	Medicine

Answers on page 64

Remember, each correct answer gives you **10 points**

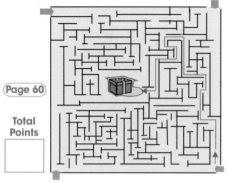

(Page 60)

Total Points

E	V	I	T	C	A	R	E	P	Y	H
S	K	S	Y	T	H	G	U	A	N	Y
C	R	N	C	F	N	A	E	T	A	T
H	O	R	E	H	C	A	E	T	F	I
T	W	D	F	Y	O	F	S	E	R	V
P	E	H	D	P	T	O	C	N	I	I
A	M	P	A	C	O	A	L	T	E	S
F	O	D	A	L	A	S	I	I	N	L
T	H	A	S	R	O	T	C	O	D	U
D	O	T	P	E	N	P	N	N	S	P
M	E	D	I	C	I	N	E	D	E	M
F	R	I	D	M	O	H	P	P	M	I

(Page 63)

Total Points

(Page 62)

Spot the 10 differences Answers

1. Girl with blue dress and brown hair has a pink flower slide in her hair
2. The alphabet has the letters e Ff missing on the blackboard
3. Girl with blue dress and brown hair has pink painted nails
4. Girl with blue dress and brown hair has a ribbon decoration around the bottom of her dress
5. Boy with blue t-shirt has pockets on his trousers
6. Boy with blue t-shirt has blue eyes
7. Boy with blue t-shirt has eyebrows
8. Girl with blonde hair has pink sleeves on her purple dress
9. Girl with purple dress now has longer blonde hair
10. Boy with ginger hair has a red t-shirt

Total Points

(Page 59)

Answers for the Quiz

1. Attention Deficit Hyperactivity Disorder
2. B. False
3. Fidgety, talks a lot, butts into games – see page 35 for more
4. B. False
5. Home, school, football ground, supermarket, birthday party etc
6. Greet with a smile, share toys in games, don't call names. see pages 49-51
7. B. False
8. Methylphenidate
9. Medicine for ADHD helps certain chemicals in the brain to get back to normal levels and improve behaviour
10. Be kind to friends and family, don't disturb others in the classroom

Total Points

Grand Total =

Everything a child needs to know about ADHD

By Dr C R Yemula
Published by ADDISS, UK
2nd edition, 2007

Written for children aged 6-12 years, this colourful book is packed with fun, humour and essential facts about ADHD.

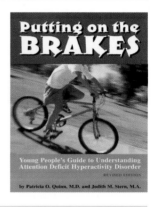

Putting on the Brakes – Young People's Guide to Understanding ADHD

By Patricia Quinn M.D.
and Judith Stern M.A.
Published by Magination Press, American Psychological Association 2002

Learning to Slow Down and Pay Attention – A book for kids about ADHD

Written by Kathleen G. Nadeau, Ph.D.
and Ellen B. Dixon, Ph.D.

Published by Magination Press, American Psychological Association, 2002

Websites and Contacts

ADDISS is a national ADHD Support Group in the UK. ADDISS provides support for parents, professionals and people affected by ADHD.

ADDISS
PO Box 340
Edgware
Middlesex
HA8 7BJ

Helpline number: 020 8952 2800
Email: info@addiss.co.uk

Useful websites

www.addiss.co.uk

www.adders.org

www.mkadhd.co.uk

www.livingwithadhd.co.uk